B

Innovative Programs for the New Senior

Beyond Bingo:
Innovative Programs for the New Senior

Sal Arrigo, Jr.

Ann Lewis

Hank Mattimore

Venture Publishing, Inc.

State College, PA

Cover Design: Sikorski Design
Production: Bonnie Godbey
Manuscript Editing: Richard Yocum
Printing and Binding: Sheridan Books, Inc.

Library of Congress Catalogue Card Number 92-82884
ISBN 0-910251-58-4

Introduction
Page ix

1

Services for Seniors
Page 1

Community Services
Page 11

2

3

Intergenerational Programs
Page 19

Fund Raising
Page 29

4

5

Crazy Ideas
Page 37

*Programs for
Seniors at Risk*
Page 45

6

7

*Programming for the
50-60 Generation*
Page 53

Afterword
Page 62

v

THE AUTHORS WISH TO ACKNOWLEDGE

the following people for their contributions to our book. Without them, *Beyond Bingo* would only be a dream.

To all the active members of the California Park and Recreation Society who shared a moment in many of our ideas; to all the senior citizens in Fairfield, Manteca, Rancho Cordova and Sacramento, CA, thanks for providing us an opportunity to perfect our trade; and to Colleen who made sure we minded our P's and Q's.

Sal Arrigo, Jr.

Born in Brooklyn, NY, Sal Arrigo, Jr. has been in the aging field since 1982. Sal Is currently the Director of the Cordova Senior Center, Sacramento, CA. He is also the author of a senior center journal, a weekly column for the Grapevine Independent newspaper. Sal has a Master's Degree in Leisure Services and a Certificate of Gerontology. He also received the California Park & Recreation President's Award in 1990.

Ann Lewis

Born in Canada and the mother of two sons, Ann Lewis has worked in the field of aging for seven years. Ann is currently a recreation supervisor for the City of Manteca, CA. She assisted in the development of senior programs and policies prior to the opening of the Manteca Senior Center and has been directly responsible for the center's day-to-day operation since 1988. Ann has a Bachelor of Arts degree in Recreation Administration from California State University at Long Beach and has worked in a variety of recreation settings in public, nonprofit, and private sectors.

Hank Mattimore

Born in Buffalo, NY, Hank Mattimore has been in the aging field since 1975. He was the Executive Director of a four-county Agency on Aging prior to his present stint as director of the Fairfield, CA Senior Center. He is a published freelance writer and, for the past five years, has written a column on aging for the Senior Spectrum newspaper and a number of other Northern California newspapers.

OVER THE HILL AND AWAY WE GO!

A new generation of Americans is striding towards their golden years, and they expect much more from recreation professionals and senior activity directors than oldies sing-a-longs and bingo. Those in charge of senior citizen programs, whether at senior centers, retirement residences, or city recreation departments, find themselves in the fastest growing (and fastest changing) area in the leisure service field. In *Beyond Bingo: Innovative Programs for the New Senior*, we have tried to write a practical, hands-on guidebook for those people who develop successful programs for, and with, this new breed of seniors.

If you have worked in the field of aging for a while, you are familiar with nutrition programs, fitness classes, health screening services, and the like. These areas are proven winners and will likely be as needed tomorrow as they are today. But have you considered providing teleconferencing support groups for homebound elderly? What about linking isolated seniors through computer networks or making ATMs available at your senior center? The first chapter of *Beyond Bingo* looks at some of the fascinating services that are being offered by recreation professionals eager to keep pace with the new senior.

However, we would be shortsighted if we focus all our efforts on providing programs and services *for* seniors. The new seniors have been moved by paraphrasing the clarion call of John

F. Kennedy, and they, too, continue to ask, "What can we do for our community?" For this reason, Chapter 2 of our guidebook is devoted to ways the recreation professional might tap the experience and wisdom of older people in the service of their communities. One senior center sponsors preretirement workshops. Another furnishes the local police department with teddy bears for their police cars; when small children become innocent victims to a crime and have to be taken from their homes, they are a little less frightened when they have a soft teddy bear to hug.

Chapter 3 directs your attention to a number of intergenerational program ideas you may want to try. Whether it's hosting a "kids day" at a senior craft shop, seniors answering letters to Santa, or sharing their life experience with local schools, there are a myriad of ways the senior recreation leader can bring the generations together. A senior center in northern California has been built on the same grounds as a junior high school. That's the kind of daring initiative that will stir the imagination of the new senior.

Whether you represent a profit-making business, a public agency, or a private nonprofit one, chances are you will be called upon to raise at least some of your budget. In Chapter 4, we have tried to put a little fun into your fund raising by suggesting some off-the-wall ideas that have raised a laugh as well as some of that green stuff. A few ideas, like hosting a "Dinner at the City Dump" may seem bizarre but, trust us, they can work. If you find yourself in a more conservative setting, don't worry. We have some straight fund raising ideas, too.

Part of our reason for putting this guide-book together is to stretch your minds—to think the unthinkable—to try what has never been tried before. While some of our zany ideas surface throughout the book, we thought we would dedicate Chapter 5 to proposing a few of our nuttier suggestions. They are the type of ideas that surface readily during many social gatherings. These ideas, modified by the age range and/or other limitations of your group, can provide offbeat and exciting events, all in a decidedly lighthearted vein.

On the more serious side, Chapter 6 is de-voted to services you may want to consider for the more frail seniors in your client population. Adult Day Care, Respite Programs, Bereave-ment Services, and a variety of support groups should be part of any service system for seniors.

Finally, in the last chapter, we have ad-dressed directly some of our thoughts on how best to attract the younger senior to our pro-grams. John Kraut, in his landmark national study on Senior Centers In America, pointed out that attracting the 50-60 year old is a problem shared by senior center directors nearly every-where. In this last chapter, we have presented to you some successful strategies for involving the younger element of the senior population.

The new senior, for example, may identify more closely with the sounds of early rock-'n'-roll than the big band music so loved by a previous generation of senior citizens.

We hope you enjoy reading *Beyond Bingo.* In putting together this book, we have called upon a combined 32 years of experience in senior programs. But, in a sense, this guidebook was written not just by ourselves, but by all the senior program people who have attended our seminars in California over the last three years. We acknowledge their contributions and hope they will continue to make suggestions and share ideas—who knows, *Beyond Bingo 2* might be hovering beyond our horizon.

1

Services for Seniors

Talking Back to Your TV and Other Programs That Go Beyond Bingo

A NEW GENERATION OF SENIORS demands more from its senior center than cards, pot luck dinners, and tired old sing-alongs of 1930-era songs. To grab the attention of these new seniors, we need to involve them, to make them participators with us in creating imaginative programs in tune with the 90s. At the same time, we have to stretch our services beyond the walls of our centers to reach those frail elderly people who are no longer able to leave their homes.

Below, we have chosen a select number of creative program ideas that we think are on target for our changing times. Maybe they will whet your appetite to go way beyond "what we did last year" and to launch your own senior programs into the 21st century. Good Luck!

TELECONFERENCING PROGRAM FOR HOMEBOUND ELDERLY

Business professionals have used teleconferencing for years. It's a practical way to interact with their colleagues all over the country without the expense of bringing everyone physically to the same place. The senior center in Fairfield, California, is using the same technology to put dozens of homebound elderly in touch with one another. Dubbed "Party Line" (with a tip of the hat to days gone by when people often shared the same telephone line), the Fairfield program was launched in November 1991 through a grant from California's Telecommunication Education Trust.

Teleconferencing equipment installed in the senior center enables up to nine people at a time to carry on a conversation with one another and with the Party Line operator. The operator's job is to welcome callers aboard and to make sure that everybody has a chance to talk. The operator also serves as an information resource by letting callers know about upcoming events or items of interest.

Most senior centers are concerned with how to get more seniors to their centers. Party Line does just that by reaching out to the neediest group of seniors, those who are trapped in their homes and consequently lack the stimulation that only social interaction can give.

Start-up costs for the Fairfield Party Line included $13,000 for the teleconferencing equipment and installation of ten telephone lines. Monthly line charges run about $30.00 per line. A part-time paid staff person operates the line, recruits new participants, organizes them into small groups, and schedules weekly conference calls.

While the expense of initiating a teleconference program in your area may seem high, it is the most cost-effective way we know of reaching the hidden elderly. As one such Fairfield caller put it, "That weekly chat is something I really look forward to. I've made friends with people I never would have had the chance to meet. Hooray for Party Line!"

By the way, once the teleconferencing equipment is installed, you may find other uses for it. For example, you can arrange weekly conference calls with other senior program people in your area, or conference calls with your senior advisory board on some urgent matter. The possibilities are endless.

If you want to know more about setting up your own Party Line, contact Chuck Warren at the Fairfield Senior Center, 1000 Webster St., Fairfield, CA 94533, or give him a call at (707) 428-7421.

"LET'S DO BREAKFAST AT THE SENIOR CENTER"

It's a simple idea, but just different enough to catch on. Offering breakfast at your senior center or senior residence can attract people you will never get for lunch. Seniors living alone love the idea of not having to make their own breakfast. The woman who has been cooking scrambled eggs for her husband for fifty years may have similar sentiments. Breakfast at a reasonable cost also attracts younger working people who like home cooking in an informal setting. These folks are your future seniors and also potential donors to your program. If you have an extra room somewhere, you might even entice one of the local service clubs to hold their weekly meeting at your center. This makes a little profit and a lot of goodwill.

Breakfast is one of the least expensive and least difficult meals to prepare. If you buy in bulk and use mostly volunteer labor, you can offer people a full country breakfast, with juice and coffee included, for a couple of dollars. If you want to make it a fund raiser, charge an extra dollar.

But the real benefit of offering breakfast is the socialization it affords to seniors living alone *and* the way it attracts community people to your center. Breakfast at the center . . . a good social service and excellent marketing, too.

THE COMPUTER CONNECTION

If your retirement residence or senior center doesn't offer computer classes, it's time to start. As our society becomes more and more computerized, computer illiterates will feel isolated and out of the mainstream. One of the most intelligent and useful services you can offer older clients is to teach them how to use this crucial piece of technology. A computer-literate older person will feel more competent and confident that he or she will survive in our changing world.

A working knowledge of the personal computer can open up new worlds to the elderly. Ownership of a personal computer (PC) and a modem (*mo*dulator-*dem*odulator, an electronic device to transmit data to or from a computer via telephone lines) can put homebound seniors in touch with other seniors in their community and computer users of all ages throughout the country. Through their computer and a program like Prodigy® (one of many telecommunication software services available), the most isolated seniors can chat with people of similar interests anywhere, anytime. They can also shop, pay bills, invest in stocks, and perform countless important tasks.

Many of you might be familiar with the international computer network called SeniorNet,[SM] which was established for older computer users. Founded a few years ago in San Francisco, SeniorNet[SM] now links older adults all over the country and in several foreign countries as well. *To know more, give SeniorNet[SM] a call at (415) 750-5030, or write to: SeniorNet,[SM] 399 Arguello Boulevard, San Francisco, CA 94118.*

Incredibly, some senior center directors think that their clients "are not ready" for computers. Baloney! Computers are increasingly user-friendly and more reasonably priced, too. Buy one for your center or get it donated. Find yourself a volunteer teacher or request one from your local adult education school and get cracking. We guarantee it will be your most popular class. One further tip—offer a second class in the evening for working seniors. They like the idea of learning with others in the same age bracket, and your senior center will gain some good community contacts.

SENIOR CENTERS ... ONE-STOP CONVENIENCE FOR OLDER PEOPLE

Anyone who has worked with seniors for a while knows that just "getting around" can be a major problem. The old-old (85 and up) lose their driving licenses. Local public transit never does quite fit the bill. So, if seniors can manage to get to your senior center, you owe them the favor of locating as many services as possible under one roof.

Most centers already offer things like a daily lunch and blood pressure screening, but there is much more you can do. Some senior centers have made arrangements with their local utility companies to be a branch office where people can settle their bills on the spot. Others simply offer a locked box labeled "Pay your utility bill here." The utility rep comes by the center twice weekly and collects the checks. The same can be done for water or phone bills. It's a simple service, but one that seniors really appreciate.

At least one senior center we are aware of is also exploring the idea of having an ATM (automated-teller machine) installed at their senior center. Why not? Another has been talking to a locally owned bank to see if there is a way a branch office can be set up at the senior center. A number of senior centers already offer stamp machines furnished by the postal service in their lobbies. Most also arrange to have a mailbox and a coin-operated newspaper box right outside their centers. It goes without saying that senior centers and residences should offer copiers and fax machines for their clients. Again, the whole idea is to provide service to our people—as much service as we can squeeze under one roof.

TALKING BACK TO YOUR TV ... ONE MORE WAY TO REACH THE HOMEBOUND

With cable television and a touch-tone phone, older people in Fairfield, California, can find out what's on the menu for lunch at the senior center, or what number to call for homemaker services, or if there is an Alzheimer's support group in town—all without leaving home. Funded through a Telecommunications Education Trust grant, the Fairfield program is the first of its kind to use the technology of interactive television to reach out to homebound older persons.

Here's how it works. For four hours daily, residents tune to the local cable channel to see a telephone number flash on their screens, and they are invited to dial it for information of interest to senior citizens. Once they dial the indicated phone number, a menu of services appears on their own television set. It may look something like this:

Welcome to the Senior Information Service. To learn more about any of the services listed below, please press the appropriate number on your telephone. Then watch your TV screen for the information.

1. **Health services offered at the Senior Center**
2. **Weekly menu for senior lunch program**
3. **Special transportation services for seniors**
4. **Support groups in the community**
5. **Housing resources for seniors**

There may be as many as ten major headings for senior services, each with its own group of subheadings. Seniors will be guided through the menu by directions flashed on their own TV, (e.g., "If you would like to know more about the Alzheimer's Support Group in this area, please press 2 on your touch-tone phone."

The interactive TV project in Fairfield began in January 1992. Initially, it is accessible only to English-speaking persons. But, eventually, it will meet the needs of homebound Spanish-speaking elders and will even be voice-activated so that visually impaired people will be able to use it.

For more information on the cost of establishing an interactive TV outreach program in your community, drop Chuck Warren a line at the Fairfield Senior Center, 1000 Webster St., Fairfield, CA 94533, or give him a call at (707) 428-7421.

SENIOR TO SENIOR SHARING OR ... "YOU-ALL C'MON OVER, HEAR?"

Sure, it's just a folksy little program, but it can do wonders for fostering camaraderie among a number of neighboring centers or residences and give senior program staff some great new ideas. I'm talking about senior centers organizing trips to other senior centers. These neighborly visits are becoming increasingly popular in California.

The visits are easy to organize. Simply call a neighboring senior center or residence and tell them your folks would like to visit their place. Chances are, they will be delighted to have you visit. It works best if you can drop by for lunch. That way, your seniors get to talk one-on-one with their se-

niors in a congenial atmosphere. Afterwards, their staff or volunteers can give your people a tour of their facility. It's amazing how you can learn something from every senior center, and it's a pleasant, inexpensive senior trip.

Some senior centers have tried variations of the simple visit by arranging to have progressive pot luck dinners or lunch. Some seniors stop for lunch at one center and then join with their seniors for a visit to a third center. Another alternative which has more appeal to armchair tourists has been tried by some California centers. One center will make a video of one of the programs or services they are particularly proud of. Then they send it on to a neighboring center with a request to add a video of one of their favorite services and to send the video on to a third center, and so on. When the video returns to the first center, it (and vicariously, the seniors) will have "traveled" to a number of other centers without having to leave home base.

For seniors who do like to travel, another idea along these lines is to link your local traveling group with some of the national and international senior hospitality programs that are becoming popular throughout the country. The idea is that seniors from this country can save a lot of money and have a better time if they can have lodging in the homes of fellow seniors who live out-of-state or abroad. A type of bed and breakfast for seniors, it sure saves on expensive hotel costs.

If you wish to pursue this more adventuresome type of senior-to-senior visit, you may want to contact the Evergreen / Travel Club, 404 North Galena Ave., Suite L-20, Dixon, IL, 60601 or call the director, Ms. Patricia Wilson, at (815) 288-9600. Evergreen charges an annual membership fee of $40 ($50 for a couple). The membership fee buys you a directory of over 1000 members with whom your seniors can stay overnight and have a full breakfast for only $10 per night per person for a single room (or $15 for a twin).

HONORING OUR ELDERS ... THE GOLDEN ANNIVERSARY BRUNCH

When Mom and Dad reach that golden anniversary date, family members just naturally want to throw a party to celebrate. That's fine as far as it goes, but at least one senior center in California feels that a private celebration is not enough. Every year, Fairfield California has a big public celebration at its senior center for *all* their citizens who have been married fifty years or more.

The city's Golden Anniversary Brunch is a special day, and it's a first-class affair with formal invitations, cloth napkins, corsages for the ladies, candlelight, champagne, musical entertainment, and an elegant Sunday brunch. The invited guests are treated like VIPs, as they well are.

The mayor and city council members make it a point to be present at this special event honoring the city's oldest and most solid citizens. Besides the music and speeches, the

Golden Anniversary Brunch usually features some light entertainment. One year, the guests were invited to play the "Oldywed" version of the "Newlywed Game." Another time, there was a fashion show featuring the gowns of the thirties and forties. On still another occasion, a minister was on hand to witness the couples renewing their marriage vows.

The "oldyweds" themselves are always asked to participate by sharing memories of how they first met, their honeymoon, those first years of marriage, etc. Naturally, there's a wedding cake, and at some point in the festivities the musicians play the anniversary waltz while the older couples dance. Schmaltzy? Sure it is, but after fifty years of marriage, who cares? Incidentally, the annual event is not limited to couples. Widows and widowers are invited, too, as long as they were married for fifty years before their spouse passed away.

The Golden Anniversary Brunch in Fairfield draws from 40 to 50 people every year and has become a hallowed tradition. It's one of those rare happenings that gives everyone, city officials, volunteers, senior center staff and honorees, the warm fuzzies. It's a win-win all around. Give it a try.

2 *Community Services*

A SENIOR CENTER IS AN INTEGRAL part of the community it serves. It does not stand alone. It is in a dependent cooperative relationship with many elements of its surroundings; its governing bodies, local businesses, sponsors, and participants. And, as in any relationship, it must give something back in order for the relationship to survive. The senior center therefore, must be seen as a "giving place."

It is easy for us as professionals to give to our clients. We are in the business of providing services and opportunities. But is this really enough? Do we not have an obligation to give back something tangible to the community in which we reside? Yes, it can be argued that we do give something back by providing services to our participants. But how much of this is really seen or felt by our neighbors?

More importantly, for many of our participants the reward of making, teaching, helping, or visiting someone else makes life worth living. The adage, "It is better to give than to receive" is a heartfelt ideal ingrained through a lifetime. The satisfaction gained from giving can take many shapes. Not everyone can or wants to volunteer at the senior center just as not everyone has the talent to make a lap robe or the stability to paint a graffiti-strewn wall. The opportunities for service must be as varied as our clients and as broad as our community's needs. In short, community service can, and should, be developed into a program unto itself.

START SLOWLY...

The words "community service" often conjure up grandiose ideas of large-scale time and energy consuming big impact projects. Consequently, community service projects are shoved aside as impossible tasks. However, community service projects do not have to be that way. There are many short-term projects that, when divided up into small pieces among a group of individuals, can be accomplished in no time. Starting slowly with these smaller types of community service projects has several added advantages. They are easier to "sell." They provide for individual and group gratification in a short amount of time with minimal commitment. They are often easy to orchestrate. In addition, a big splash can be made with just a little publicity effort.

Receipts, Receipts, Receipts

Many supermarket chains are offering incentive campaigns for schools to earn computers, books, etc. Your senior center can adopt a school and help to collect receipts. This is virtually a no commitment project for the center and/or your seniors. Your participants simply bring receipts when they come in your door and place them in a box provided by the school. Keep tabs on the dollar value of the receipts and report in your newsletter, etc.

Preemie Caps

Everyone has a soft spot in their hearts for newborn babies. Offer an opportunity to serve a hospital and premature infants by providing temperature stabilizing "preemie caps." These can be made from tubes of soft stretchable fabric or can be knitted with soft yarn.

Teddy Bear Connection

Unfortunately, it is inevitable that members of the police force will be faced with negative situations involving children. Whether the incident is a car accident, child abuse, or domestic violence, a simple teddy bear can go a long way in provid-

ing comfort and in developing trust between the child and the officer. Many senior centers in California have taken on the task of making bears for each local patrol car. The relationship provides the child in need with something to hang on to, while the police department is provided with an ongoing source of teddy bears.

The task of making the bears can be divided among individual seniors or can be a group assembly line process. Suitable fabric oftentimes can be gathered from the project participants themselves. Stuffing and patterns are available at local fabric or variety stores (and many times the source will donate these goods if you explain the project). Remember that eyes and other features should be painted on or very securely fastened so that a small child will not swallow them.

Environmental Messengers

Recycling and environmental concern is not a new movement. Seniors have expert knowledge to share in this arena. Team up with local Earth Day and/or Arbor Day committees to have a format in which to share how to make a biodegradable compost heap, the total range of recyclable products down to foil and batteries, and what flowers can act as natural pesticides for the vegetable garden. Your seniors may even want to get the message across by making and dressing up in costumes such as an aluminum can or Woodsy Owl. Your involvement will be very welcome and you can even make a penny or two by collecting recyclables or selling refreshments.

ONE STEP AT A TIME . . .

For some, community service rewards may come from providing a more personal type of gift through the sharing of knowledge as well as time. In developing community service projects, the needs of this type of senior may provide the avenue for the first steps outside your own four walls without requiring an overabundance of your own time.

Grandparents and Books

The California State Library system utilizes senior volunteers to introduce the world of books to youth of all ages. They provide basic training in storytelling/story reading and help volunteers choose age-appropriate materials. The volunteers are then scheduled during afterschool and evening hours to read to children at the library, at day-care centers, etc. If your library does not have such a program, a local librarian or school teacher may be willing to help train volunteers. Your help in recruiting volunteers and keeping tab of volunteer time will link this program to your facility.

Speakers Bureau

A world of knowledge abounds within the heart and soul of every senior center. Participants come to us with work skills, life skills, travel experience and hobbyist enthusiasm. Tapping and organizing this resource is the foundation for a speakers bureau. Putting together a catalog of this expertise will invite inquiries for speakers to bring history alive in the classroom, spice up a service organization meeting, and jazz up the local crafts fair with a working exhibit.

As an added bonus, the next time a speaker you've scheduled for the senior center doesn't show up or you're asked to speak, but have a conflict, you will know who can pinch hit.

Patriotic Spirit

Our country is never without a protective force even in times of peace and our servicemen and women should always feel the support of the nation they believe in. Adopting a unit of the young people who are currently serving us can be a great community service project. It will foster friendships, provide moral support, and bring a sense of purpose to a long day. Having those that have served the nation in the past recount their experiences and make comparisons or ask questions through letters about new technology invites a sharing of historical and technical expertise. Firsthand knowledge of

long forgotten cravings or rationed goods may provide the basis for the best care package ever received. If your center is close to a military installation, an invitation to lunch may make those far from home feel more welcome.

THE TOUGHER STUFF

Service projects have a way of becoming contagious. You may find this "bug" spreading among your project participants and/or have community members at large seeking your services for larger and larger projects. It may take a little effort to evaluate the projects that are right for you and to meet the needs of those concerned, but you can become the healers of graffiti-strewn walls, the consciousness-raisers of the community, and the support givers and teachers of tomorrow's generation.

Graffiti Abatement

As our cities grow, we inadvertently provide a canvas for graffiti. The miles of sound walls, freeway overpasses, public transportation vehicles, and business buildings constantly cry out for new paint to cover the protests, love notes, and gang signatures bestowed upon them. Only an organized and constant battle plan seems to keep up with and discourage the problem.

Abatement programs have taken different shapes in different towns. In one city, senior police patrol officers report problems to the local Boys Club to eradicate on a weekly basis. In another, senior graffiti busters have set up a call-in line and have organized a phone tree among the painting crew. In yet another town, walls are adopted by senior and service clubs to keep clean. And in others, art groups fund mural projects to cover the most abused surfaces to make them a source of pride for the neighborhood. All this takes organization and money, but community pride is a powerful force. Many cities and state governments are now budgeting for graffiti removal and/or have "Art in Public Places" grants available to fund those mural projects.

Plays With Purpose

Does your senior center have a drama group or a few people with a flair for acting waiting to be in the spotlight? Is there an issue that needs to be addressed and/or a message you want to send to your community? You can teach those lessons with a little creative help and cultivate or nurture talent at the same time by presenting "plays with a purpose."

One community in California recently wrote, directed, made props for, and acted in a series of vignettes addressing crime prevention and senior abuse issues. The skits, targeted at the senior audience, were videotaped for use by the Department of Justice for community awareness programs throughout the state. The group has now considered developing a show to heighten awareness of patient rights. Other ideas that have been tossed around have included: audience participation plays that demonstrate what it is like to experience the disabilities associated with old age, a series of reminiscing videos related to local history, and puppet shows based on American folk tales.

As with other service projects, a group of dedicated individuals is essential to developing these theatrical productions. The group must be led by someone with a knack for blending diverse personalities into a cohesive unit while allowing individual strengths to soar. The project must remain focused and time frames for completion established. Costs can be kept to a minimum with a little scrounging and forums for presentation can be established by developing working relationships with senior clubs, schools, nursing homes, etc.

Latchkey Programs

With the abundance of single parent families and the necessity for many families to have both parents working to make ends meet, quality child care for school age children is a dire need in many communities. In those same communities, the senior center may be quiet during afterschool hours. Establishing a cost-effective latchkey program at a community-based facility may be the answer that the school around the corner is looking for. Money is available through senior employment programs to pay workers to be trained and to have them work in such environments as providers of activities, tutors, and companions. Many retired teachers or social workers may relish the opportunity to work on a limited basis with kids again, and many seniors who have never worked with kids may want a crack at it, especially for a few pennies in their pockets.

Granted, this project takes a lot of selling and a great amount of ongoing coordination and patience. Licensing may be required, equipment may need to be purchased, and policies must be generated. However, the rewards of providing a safe environment with opportunities to get expert help with homework will be a great benefit to the youngsters and parents within the senior center neighborhood.

And that's what it is all about—the neighborhood—being interdependent and caring. The senior center does not live in a vacuum. It is a vital part of the community within which it dwells and has an obligation to offer to its own participants a chance to make life worth living within the community it serves.

3 *Intergenerational Programs*

WHETHER YOU ARE THE DIRECTOR OF a senior center housed in a community center, are investigating further sources of funding, or arc cncouraging community service types of projects, you will, at some point, come up against the challenge of intergenerational activity programming. In this area of the senior center business (maybe more so than in many activity areas), how you view this challenge and how you project that viewpoint and/or strategically plan for it may make or break your efforts to succeed.

So just what is this intergenerational business all about?

Intergenerational activity programming is the art of breaking down age barriers to encourage the discovery of joy in playing and/or working with a different generation.

Intergenerational activity programming is the craft of over-coming the voices that say "We don't want kids in the senior center!," "What do they know?," and the unsaid "I'm afraid."

Intergenerational activity programming is the simplicity of a grandparent-grandchild breakfast or a mother-daughter-granddaughter fashion show and the ongoing structure and challenges of tutoring programs, home renovation projects, and day camps. Intergenerational activity *possibilities* are based on the needs of the community, the desires of your participants (younger and older), and your dreams for the future.

Intergenerational activity *keys* include building slowly, recruiting carefully, promoting vigorously, and, most importantly, finding the fun.

OVER 50 & UNDER 10

Grandparent-Grandchild Breakfast

Bring together those over 50 and under 10 by hosting a "grandparent-grandchild" theme breakfast. Ideas that have worked well include "Breakfast with Santa" and "Breakfast with the Easter Bunny." Serve breakfast buffet-style, take photographs, provide entertainment, and have a simple craft or activity. A nominal fee will cover costs, and those without grandchildren (real or adopted) are willing to volunteer just to be part of the event.

A successful intergenerational event (like all other special events) depends upon "proper prior planning." In this instance, success may be determined by planning your break-fast event at a time that does not conflict with regular senior center activities, by considering a time that is convenient for families (Saturday mornings work well), by marketing your breakfast widely through local preschools and elementary schools as well as senior news connections, and by arranging for "adoptions." Trying to keep fees at a minimum, being realistic as to how many you can serve, and keeping the event moving from one activity to another are also important. You will know that you have planned successfully when you experience the laughter that occurs when it's the grandparent's turn to hunt for Easter eggs.

Letter From Santa

A community service project with intergenerational charm is a Letter From Santa. It has been tried in a variety of ways: adopting a preschool or elementary school class, opening it to the community through press releases, and providing an opportunity to write to one's own grandchild. Recommendations include developing your own stationery, setting aside some time for group writing, and finding a source to pay for mailing (if necessary). Your assistance and guidance will be appreciated by your volunteers and by those for whom this program impacts if you also put together a sample letter to be followed, encourage some personaliza tion by answering the child's questions,  and if you refrain from using agency letterhead, envelopes, or postage markings. Above all, do not promise anything to a child in your responses. The rewards in this program are many. You will share joys and tears with each other as you receive colorful drawings, read heartwrenching tales of bad times, and realize you have provided a language exercise for second graders.

Tap Dance

You are never too old or too young to start tap dancing, so why not do it with a young man or young lady? Beginning classes seem to work best. Trust and grace (in more ways than one) are developed as the ages learn new skills together. You will need to choose your instructor carefully; it takes skill to develop a rapport within the multigenerational classroom and to have the class move at a pace comfortable to participants in varied age groups. However, the sincere hug between dance partners at the end of the class recital and the knowledge that there is an understanding of far more than dance steps between those partners are the gifts resulting from your efforts.

Kids Day at the Boutique

Kid-sized prices on handmade goods provide the basis for a gift shopping opportunity for children in a safe environment. Open the doors to your senior center boutique at a specified time, give Mom a few minutes of relaxation with a cup of coffee (in another room), and have volunteers help little and not-so-little ones shop for the special people in their lives. If you really are ambitious, you may even want to provide gift wrapping services or a "make and take" craft table.

Don't forget if you have consignment items in your boutique to make sure to check with the craftsperson regarding price, to allow children to make their own choices as much as possible, and to have plenty of change and bags to "hide" the purchases.

Everybody wins in this activity. The center and/or consignees make money, the children get quality gifts at prices they can afford, parents get a break, and volunteers know they are truly providing a community service.

Game Time

Do the great-grandchildren of your participants know how to play Parcheesi™? Do your participants know how to play the video game "Dr. Mario®?" Why not host a Game Day? Set it up round-robin fashion, recruit a few game geniuses, and bring together the generations to learn the favorite games of one another.

Some clues to success for your gaming event are to have each game station manned by an "expert" to explain the rules, to walk participants through each game, and to add a little friendly competition by offering prizes for various challenges (high score, low score, etc.). The opportunity you create with this event for future quality time between the generations will reap many benefits.

OVER 50 & 'TWEENS AND TEENS

Clean Up, Paint Up, Fix Up

Is there graffiti on the sound wall or neighborhood store? Is there a senior in need of minor home repairs? Does your center need a thorough cleaning? Senior brains and junior energy mixed with a little community spirit can make a dent in your nearest disaster area. Adoption, ownership, and pride will keep the program going.

Resources abound for funding such projects. Local service clubs, grants, designated fund raisers, and youth groups such as Boy Scouts, Key Clubs, and Rainbow Girls were founded on community service principles.

When taking on these challenging programs, be sure to clearly define the scope of the project to be undertaken, set up specific work schedules, and research funding sources. Look at the small rewards such as the sight of a nail going in straight because of a helpful hand, the perfect blending of paint, and the pride in a job well done as well as the finished project. You will have accomplished a lot.

Senior Prom

Dreams are what senior proms are made of—the anticipation of your first date at the eighth grade dance, the glamour of formal attire, the memory of the kiss on the doorstep. A senior prom provides dreams for old and young alike. Two dreams which have worked are: combining an eighth grade dance and a formal senior dance to create a "junior-senior" prom and establishing a tradition of a junior class at the high school planning a senior prom for elders.

The magic of the dreams is the setting; make it one that memories will be built on. Be sensitive to the needs of those without "dates"; don't forget the mixers and line dances. Provide music that crosses the age barrier and/or a wide variety of music. Remember that details are important here. Did you contact the florist about a reduced price or a donation of corsages? When well-planned, your prom can be the emotional experience we all remember. There will be smiles and tears and new memories and dreams of days gone by.

Music Magic

The high school music department has voices and instruments which can provide a wonderful blend with senior vocal and instrumental talent. Seniors can practice at the high school  at times the students are actually in class. Community events, such as Christmas Tree Lightings, can provide performance showcases.

In planning your musical extravaganza, the music directors of both groups must be clear as to the goals of the program, and the opportunities for both age groups to practice on their own will allow for "quirks" to be worked out in a nonthreatening manner. Be sure to obtain permission from the school administration before your senior participants show up on campus. Planned gleefully, you will start a tradition of great performances for your community.

Art Camp

Camp is a place to share, and when two talented age groups combine in a hands-on learning experience, the result is friendship. High school-aged artists can take the lead in newer art mediums such as soft sculpture and oil pastels, and the time-honored traditions of needlework and watercolor painting can be instructed by the older artists. Camp can take place in town as a one-day seminar or over the course of a week or more during a holiday break. The focus is to share a common interest, tap into the talent, experiment with the medium, and be on your way to creating new masterpieces.

Please note that this type of program has a high impact on the normal daily functioning of a senior center: plan carefully if your center is the "camp-site." Also, create an environment of positive experimentation—it's okay if the clay sculpture of a horse looks like a dog. The work (of planning) is worth the discovery of new hobbies, fresh talent, and artwork for your center.

OVER 50 & THE COLLEGE CROWD

Cars, College, and Cruising

Times have not changed so much that a night out on the town doesn't include showing off the car and the girl (or guy). Why not showcase the spectacular of then and now in an "across the ages" car show, rally, hobby information fair, and sock hop. Design creative awards to promote the mingling of, and to acknowledge the differences between, the college crowd of today and yesterday. Make this a community-sanctioned event by involving the local car club and by getting all the permits you may need. The smiles of appreciation for one another's knowledge and beautiful belongings can make this event one that is longed for as much as the items it showcases.

Writer's Workshop/Club

Creativity and talent appear to surge at each end of the adult-hood spectrum. Gathering together writers of the new college set and the horizon college set may  stimulate creative new thought, reminiscences, critical acclaim, punctuation lessons, a haiku poem, or a lengthy novel. Most likely, with only a few rules of protocol, weekly or monthly meetings for those who want to share their writing talent, and growth from the thoughts of others, will provide for exploration of new styles and a better understanding of the challenges faced by each generation.

To start a writer's group or club at your senior center, you may want to first gather your senior participants, to determine the how, when, and where of the group, and to discuss the format to keep things moving. Do you want to critique one writer weekly? Occasionally throw out a topic for an impromptu creative process? Only focus on poetry or novels? Once you have a general plan, contact the colleges targeting creative writing and English course instructors and let the word(s) fly.

Sharing the Wealth of Knowledge

The junior high school has kids with problems—the senior center has adults with great coping skills and time to listen. The high school has computer whiz kids; the senior center has skilled wood craftsmen.

You know there is a need for a talent bank, a speakers bureau, and expanded volunteer coordination—the college has students looking for Master's Degree projects and internship possibilities. Tap the potential.

ACROSS THE AGES

Mother/Daughter Fashion Show

Do you remember the pride of having your daughter ask you
to be part of the Girl Scout mother/daughter fashion show?
Do you remember thinking for the first time that your mother
was truly elegant? Do you still burst with the joy of remem-
bering your wife and daughter on stage together looking so
young and so grown up and so beautiful? Recapture those
memories with a grown-up mother/daughter fashion show.

Most boutiques and even department stores are delighted
to have their fashions displayed and often have a master of
ceremonies available, too. Make this event special by serving
afternoon tea or wine and cheese as part of the event. Orchestrate fashion partners for those who wish to participate, but
don't have a mother or daughter. Include granddaughters or
grandfather and son teams, also.

Model Train Show

Clickety clack, clickety clack . . . the lure of the railroad. It is
a sense of adventure and the rhythm of a lullaby rolled into
one. You can capture the romance of an era gone by or child-
hood memories of the train under the Christmas tree by team-
ing up with model railroad enthusiasts for a day or a weekend
event designed to show off a hobby and bring generations together.

Grandpa can share the adventure of hopping a train
across the country as he points out the differences in locomo-
tives set up on a miniature scale track. Mom can share her
creative ideas by designing a village for the Swiss Alps to be
set up in the senior center dining room. The children's eyes
will be wide with wonder as the model train engineer as-
sembles his trestle and track.

To top it off, this is a win-win event for the senior center from another perspective. You don't have to do the work! The model train club will gather the participants, set up the exhibits, and do the publicity. You can use it as a fund raiser by charging admission and selling refreshments. Held during nonbusiness hours, you will have also succeeded in intergenerational programming without impacting your regular program.

Now it's your turn. Take these beginnings and dream. Take the challenge and make it fit your community. Intergenerational activities will not shake the foundations of your program; they will become the building blocks of your program's future.

Fund Raising

YOU JUST FINISHED A STAFF MEETING with the department head, and you still can't believe your ears. In order to keep a part of your program, you must raise the necessary funds. There is a good chance we have all heard of budget horror stories and the person who has never fund raised. On occasion, we all could use some fresh ideas.

This chapter on fund raising includes such ideas as collecting pennies, mobile hair cutting, nonevents, a shopping spree, and novel approaches like a "dinner at the dump." Each idea can be adapted to your particular program. Oh, and these ideas can be fun, too! As you read along, start your brain motor and be creative. The key to any successful fund raiser is to get people involved. Show your staff and volunteers that fund raising can be fun for them and for those who contribute.

COLLECT THOSE PRESIDENT LINCOLNS

If the place that you work has a small staff and not many volunteers (or maybe you *are* the entire staff), don't worry! Find yourself a large glass jar (about the size of a pickle jar) and

place it on your reception counter. Attach a sign that reminds people about how annoying it is to carry around pennies and how this glass jar gives them an outlet into which they may dump their coins. Tell people their "two cents worth" is what you're after. Tell them they are supporting the senior program by unloading their President Lincolns! Set a goal of at least 100,000 pennies

and don't worry about counting every cent. We're sure a local bank will help you count.

MOBILE HAIR CUTTING

Let's face it—at one time or another, you have had a request for a particular kind of service that you have never heard of

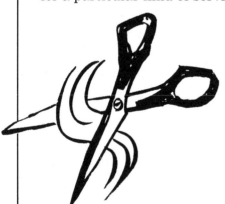

before or have never thought about incorporating into your program. As senior centers become more of a "one-stop shopping center," senior citizens are asking "so what's new?" Since the majority of your participants are probably women, you can bet most go to a beauty salon on occasion. Instead, why not bring the salon to them? Ask a local salon to assist your center

in making a few bucks. For every haircut the beautician completes, a donation is made to your center.

The beauty salon gets a little publicity, you make some money, and the seniors were served without the inconvenience of traveling to the salon. Tell the beautician you will take care of appointments and times, and, for every haircut over a set amount, the donation percentage increases (for example, 1st 5 cuts - 10%, 2nd 5 cuts - 15%, 3rd 5 cuts - 20%, etc.) You're in charge, so *you* decide how the program runs. Remember, be creative and use your imagination!

NONEVENTS

There is a little more effort required to make this a successful fund raiser, but it also can bring you lots of money. Instead of counting on people to show up for an event, "un-invite" them and ask for a contribution. There's a good chance you'll receive a contribution when the donor doesn't have to get all dressed up and listen to some boring speaker.

To start, ask your Chamber of Commerce for a list of their members. Edit it into a workable "invitation" list that fits your postage and printing budget. A guest list of 125 will cost you under $100. The payback can be 5, 6, or 7 times your start-up costs. Here are some hints: first, for the invitation, tell the prospective donor they are "un-invited" to a fund raiser that is going to help a specific program. Second, state that, for a designated amount ($15.72, $18.93, $21.21, etc.), they can reserve a seat at your party. Tell them that although they don't have to "eat that same old chicken dinner" or "sit through tiresome presentations," you do want their contribution. (Never make the contribution an even amount; this would take away from the fun aspect. Also, don't make it unreasonably high, as this would cut down on donations.) Third, pick a deadline date and send invitations out three weeks prior. You'll be amazed at how many people will send you their money and ask for more than one "reservation."

Finally, if you want to try other nonevents, think about a phantom dance, nonexistent cruise, or any make-believe event that your imagination allows you to create.

SHOPPING SPREE

This fund raiser is more involved than any of those previously discussed. It also can be one of your biggest moneymakers. To accomplish a shopping spree, our best advice is to involve another community group, preferably a youth organization. With this, you are creating a solid fund raiser as well as an intergenerational program. One idea that has proven success-ful is using your local youth baseball or softball groups. Since equipment and umpires gobble up most of their budget, a $3,000 or $4,000 fund raiser can buy new equipment that will last several seasons (which will help cut down the following year's expenses) and take care of paying for umpires.

Here are some tips for your successful shopping spree: after you have contacted an interested youth group, target a local market (not a big chain store) who is involved in support-ing their community. Ask them to sponsor a shopping spree with the youth group selling tickets to any person age 18 or over. The tickets give buyers the chance to win some fabulous prizes. Okay, you say, what's in it for me at the senior center? A breakdown of who benefits goes like this: the youth group keeps all of the ticket sale money, and the senior center gets a donation from the market when all the receipts from the shop-ping spree are counted. The donation to you is a matching of the total receipts! The market gets all the publicity from local news, ticket sales, word of mouth, and so on.

Some possible suggestions for prizes are: first prize wins a four minute shopping spree; second prize wins a two minute shopping spree; third prize gets a $50.00 store gift certificate; and fourth prize gets a $25.00 store gift certificate. Take it from us, in six minutes of a shopping spree, a total of $2,000 or more can be accumulated. This is your money for your se-nior program! You'll have to work out more of the details. For example: How many tickets should you print? Should you have music at the store for entertainment? Does the youth group operate a concession stand on the day of the spree? What time of the day is best to have your spree?

Why not try holding the spree during the morning hours possibly on a weekend when a large volume of people are in the store? It generates good publicity, and it creates more drama surrounding the event. You may also want to give out discount coupons to those shoppers who are lucky enough to have been in the store during the shopping spree. The more help you have, the more involved the spree can be and, consequently, the more money made.

Don't let a slow economy make you think some Mom and Pop store won't go for this idea. Yes, they're putting out merchandise and cash donations, but they are also attracting new business. In the long run, they are making back many times their shopping spree output. Your center is also making a solid community friend.

DINNER AT THE DUMP

Try this curious, crazy-sounding and profitable moneymaker. Curiosity will be one of your main attractions. People will come just to see if anyone can have dinner at the dump. (Actually, it is held at a recycling plant.)

If not the recycling plant, how about the water treatment, sewage plant, or other city utility company? The city of Davis, California, has made this fund raiser a top community attraction. Before you decide that we have entered the Twilight Zone with our ideas, read on.

If you are lucky enough to have a recycling plant and you receive permission to use their facility, you are on your way. Select a location at the recycling plant where tables and chairs (made of recycled material, if possible) can be set up to accommodate many people. When you accomplish this, involve fast-food chains by asking them to donate the entrees. In other words, they will cater your food at a recycling plant or other utility location! Sounds nuts, but it works. Charge a reasonable amount, line up service clubs and other volunteers to help serve, clean up, etc. The biggest reason you use a fast-food outlet is that the meal can be served in a disposable container that will make your clean up minimal.

You decide what your dinner at the dump should include. Your imagination is your only limitation!

USED CAR SALE

This is an excellent fund raiser, but a time-consuming event. The idea is to find an unused and easily accessible parking lot on a Sunday. Since most people will car shop on this day, here is your chance to help make shopping a whole lot easier. When you have found a place for this event, use the following guidelines to help make as much money as possible.

First, for those people who are looking to buy and/or sell used cars on a private basis, advertise that there is now one location where a large selection of cars will be available. Remember that the more advertising you do, the better the probable turnout. Second, each car that occupies a space in the parking lot is charged a small fee. If a car is sold, you then get a fixed percentage of the sale price. The higher the price, the higher the commission.

The authors are aware of service clubs in the state of California who use the Used Car Sale as a prime source of their service income. One final note though: check with your insurance carrier to make sure you have adequate liability coverage. After you have accomplished this, start making money!

THE MARBLE GAME

A fund raiser that can net your senior center some easy money. Take 100 marbles (95 white and 5 red) and place them in an opaque container. Sell three chances for a dollar. Each day, at lunch, draw three tickets. Those three lucky people get to pick one marble. If any one or more of them pick a red marble, they get half the take from all the ticket sales. If you have multiple winners, then divide the take equally.

If all three people pick a white marble, you discard them and roll over the ticket sales to the next day. The odds get better to win, and the prize money and senior center's share grows. You can place your own bet on the fact that the more prize money available the more tickets you'll sell.

5

Crazy Ideas

HAVE YOU EVER GOTTEN THE URGE to do something so crazy with your senior programming that you wondered if it was illegal? Do you ever want to shake up your participants with a program so off-the-wall that your sanity would be questioned? If so, try a bathing beauty contest or "show us your muscles" contest. If you want something more outrageous, why not plan for a senior dating game, sexy senior calendar, or a pet show using live and stuffed animals? Let your imagination run wild! Just make sure those involved will still have their dignity when they're through participating.

Imagine for a moment that you have a list of thousands of recreational programs geared for all age groups. You're looking over this list and you come across a program that, with a few variations, would be an exciting, well-attended event for seniors. Why? Because you have no limitations to your thinking or creativity. You won't allow yourself to be trapped in your usual thinking pattern. Finally, you have knocked down your mental barriers. You're now freewheeling; ready to take the simplest program and make it into the nuttiest program you will allow yourself. Here are some ideas to help get started on your "new" thinking.

BATHING BEAUTY CONTEST

This can be a real winner. Seniors at your center can recall the days of their youth when they brazenly "strutted their stuff." There may be one or two in your group who were the envy of the beach and very popular with the opposite sex. Who knows? One of your participants may have legs that rival Betty Grable's while another has the chest of Johnny Weissmuller. However, this bathing beauty contest doesn't show any skin at all. Instead, the participants wear their outfits over their clothes. No kidding. No one will be embarrassed by having to take anything off. The whole idea is a spoof on the beauty contest of today. There are categories for your particular show, such as worst-looking bathing suit, most colorful outfit, most graceful walk, and so on. Make up more fun rules, have some beach music playing, get a panel of judges, and, most definitely, take pictures. If there is enough help, decorate your facility with pictures of beaches, oceans, sunny skies, and possibly, Frankie and Annette!

SHOW US YOUR MUSCLES

You probably have seen pictures of senior men who, in their sixties and seventies, can give Charles Atlas a flex or two. Well, maybe we're stretching a bit, but just because one's age registers at 70 doesn't mean he/she must fit the stereotypical image of a senior citizen. What do you suppose the reaction would be if you start your publicity for this "muscles" event? Curiosity? Intrigue? Lunacy? We'll bet the local workout places will raise an eyebrow or two when you ask to place your advertising flyer in their facility! You're now helping to educate other generations by letting the "20-year-old stud" know that he isn't the only good-looking muscle-bound fella.

Okay, here are some hints to get started. Anyone 60 years of age or better can enter. Participants will be judged on the size of their muscles when flexed. A note here: the judge(s) should be a man/woman, preferably some good-looking aerobic instructor(s). Hey, it's fine to give those participating and those watching a chance to raise their blood pressure a few points! You'll get laughs, blushing seniors, and people telling you over and over, "you're crazy!"

Give a set of dumbbells as top prize. You make the call. Don't be bashful to put on such a show. You can bet most of your audience has seen or heard more risqué programs on everyday television.

SENIOR DATING GAME

You probably have seen or heard of the "Dating Game" show that aired on television many years ago. It was a way for young people to meet a member of the opposite sex, and sometimes this meeting developed into a marriage. Following a similar format, why not try a "Senior Dating Game"? How many older people go out to dinner by themselves? How many wish they could go to the theater, but due to some constraint (no transportation, feelings of insecurity in a large crowd, etc.), they pass up a chance to get out of the house?

The Dating Game format is fairly simple. The individual who would like to go on a date presents 6 to 8 inquiring questions to at least three potential "dates," who are hidden from the questioner's view. The person asking the questions may

want to cover such categories as hobbies, interests, height, weight, color of eyes/hair, etc. After several minutes for each "date" to get a fair shot at answering each question, the questioner then selects his/her choice. Encourage the audience to assist with the individual's choice. In other words, let the audience hoot and holler and, of course, applaud the selection. Now, for this "dream date," arrange dinner for two, transportation, corsages, and boutonnieres. Play it up! You may be surprised at how many seniors will participate. This is a fun event that can only get your senior organization the title of "Senior Dating Capital of the County"!

SEXY SENIOR CALENDAR

Here's an idea that will turn some heads and be a hot topic of conversation. If you have seen an exercise videotape featuring women 55 years and older, then you'll know a sexy senior calendar will be a hit. We're sure you have seen or heard about *Playboy* magazine's monthly calendar pinups. Well, this activity is based on the same principles (except your people do keep their clothes on). Eventually, you can turn this idea into a fund raiser by selling the calendars. However, for now you'll have your work cut out for you by just getting past those "crazy idea" naysayers.

This idea has several options. You can select men or women and photograph only their faces, shoot from the waist up, or photograph the entire individual. As part of your publicity campaign, anyone who wants to take a shot at being a "cover man or woman" can participate. Age requirement can start at 55 years old and up. Perhaps it is possible to arrange for a local photographer to donate time to this project. Also, a local printing house might manufacture the finished calendar at a reduced cost, or perhaps you can convince them to donate their services. Think ahead and imagine how elegant your calendar will be. Sure, it may take time to produce, but it can also be a great selling tool to introduce more of the community to your other programs.

There is a good chance many seniors will participate. Arrange for a panel of judges to pick the best photos and go with that. Maybe you'll want four face photos, four face-to-waist photo's and four full-length photos. It's your program and imagination. Why should *Playboy* have all the fun?

DOG AND CAT SHOW

What's so special about a dog and cat show? Well, this show features both live *and* stuffed animals! After all, some seniors may not be capable of housing live animals, so why exclude them from the fun? Again, choose a panel of judges to determine prizewinners in both the live and stuffed categories. Let people have as many entries as they wish and then, after the show, throw a pot luck dinner.

A few words of caution, though—seniors should keep pets on a leash or in a pet cage. If the pets happen to break loose, you'll be chasing them all over your center and, well, you may be needing your maintenance crew to help clean up some messes.

Also, use the opportunity to provide some pet education to the older person. Some suggested topics are grooming, feeding, and vaccination schedules. If you allow for a question and answer session, you'll be providing both the pet and pet owner a valuable opportunity to have a long, healthful relationship.

OLDER WOMEN ... YOUNGER ESCORTS

You have more women attending your center, right? Yes, probably lots more women. Do you know something? Some of these single ladies would like nothing better than the experience of dressing up and being escorted once more to a dinner

or dance by a gentleman. They don't necessarily want to get married, for pete's sake. They just like the idea of having a male companion for an evening. Well, if you live near a college, or better still, a military installation, why not recruit some young single men to act as escorts for a night out with your single, female participants?

It's not as far-fetched as it may seem. Some of these young guys are far from home and kind of lonely themselves. They enjoy the idea of doing a good deed and some of them end up having as much fun as their dates. Talk to the commanding officer's staff at a military base or the community services person at a college. Sure, maybe the whole idea sounds a little off-the-wall, but before you knock it, ask your female participants what they think of the idea. We'll bet *they* don't knock it.

COMEDY HOUR

Seniors learn to live with physical pain, economic hardship, loss of spouse, loss of status—you name it. Old age isn't for sissies. That's why it's important to bring an old-fashioned belly laugh or two into their lives. Your senior center could schedule a weekly comedy hour to take participants' minds off their losses and troubles.

How does it work? Seniors are invited to bring a joke, a silly story, or a crazy skit and share it with fellow seniors at the weekly get-together. People are encouraged to be as creative and nutty as they like. Nothing is too outrageous. You can dress like a clown, wear a funny hat, sing a song—whatever. Sometimes they'll play audiocassettes of old radio shows like Jack Benny and Fred Allen, or simply read jokes from Reader's Digest. It doesn't make a heck of a difference what you do. If people are in the mood to laugh, they will. For that short period at least, troubles melt away, and the problems of aging are forgotten. A comedy hour . . . not a bad way to lighten up staff and participants alike. Give it a whirl at your center.

We hope that you'll try one of our crazy ideas or a variation using your unlimited imagination. Your senior program and your senior participants can only be worthy benefactors.

6 *Programs for Seniors at Risk*

SURE, IT'S FUN TO PLAN TRIPS TO LAS Vegas or Atlantic City or to organize a senior Jeopardy game. However, senior recreation professionals are especially challenged by the basic human needs of the frail elderly, older people who can no longer go on trips or dance or participate in the senior Olympics. At one time, they could do all those things. They wish they still could. But now, mentally or physically disabled, hobbled by the losses of age, they are dependent and count on us for the services that will help them to survive.

Of all the segments of the senior population, it is for these seniors "at risk" that we must go "beyond bingo" in providing services to them. For these vulnerable at risk older people, a professionally run senior center is not just a convenience; it is a necessity. Feeling most at home in our centers or residential facilities, they naturally turn to us for solid information, counseling, and help in getting the assistance they need.

There are a large number of programs and services that will be especially helpful to the more frail seniors in your community. Certainly, every senior center should offer at least the following:

1) *A strong information and referral component.*
    Seniors have a right to expect that their local senior center has current, accurate information on services and programs relevant to their situation.

2) *Educational workshops and programs that help elders and their families find their way through the confusing labyrinth of health and social services.*
    At your center or residential facility people should be able to find professional presentations on living trusts, wills, Medicare/Medicaid, tips on choosing a good nursing home, patient rights, supplemental insurance options, and much more.

3) *Direct health and social services, such as blood pressure and diabetes screening, hearing and vision testing, both congregate and home delivery meal programs, shopping assistance, and some type of legal and tax assistance.*
    Tax assistance is usually available through the AARP Senior Tax Aide Program.
    Legal assistance can sometimes be obtained through your local Area Agency on Aging. The

senior center in Fairfield, California, has had a legal assistance program for many years through the generosity of local attorneys. On a rotation basis, once a month, lawyers donate a two-hour time period in which they offer 30-minute consultations. It's not too much of a burden on any one attorney and the seniors reap the benefit of having attorneys at the center.

Two other direct services are telephone reassurance programs and postal alert services. The telephone reassurance program, often know as Phone-A-Friend, is a person-to-person service intended for shut-ins. Volunteers, matched on a one-to-one basis with home bound seniors, call their clients daily at a prearranged time just to make sure they are okay. Normally, the service is provided by older volunteers and is free. Some centers use a high-tech version of Phone-A-Friend by programming a computer to do the calling.

Postal Alert Programs, usually cosponsored by a senior center and the local post office, uses to its advantage the one person who makes a daily stop at the door of almost every elderly person. The mail carrier is in a position to know immediately when there is something amiss. He or she notices when a person isn't picking up mail or when newspapers are collecting around the door. As part of this program, the mail carrier will then notify the senior center or the agency with whom arrangements have been made in advance.

4) *Transportation.*

It is futile to offer a variety of services to our most vulnerable clients without providing them access to our facility. Younger seniors have no difficulty getting to our programs, whether by private vehicle or by using public transportation. The frail elderly, by definition, need additional help. Some senior centers have set up their own volunteer driver programs to take care of this

need. Others are able to tap into publicly funded paratransit programs. Whatever the method used, a center is not providing for its most needy clients unless it offers them a practical way of accessing their services.

5) *Support groups, both for seniors needing help and for their caregivers or family members.*

Some senior centers offer as many as a dozen support groups for everything from the caregivers of Alzheimer's patients to elders who recently lost a spouse to seniors afflicted with loss of vision late in life.

There are support groups for people with emphysema, diabetes, muscular dystrophy, alcoholism, and many more. (There is even one senior center that has a very popular support group for "pack rats," people who collect everything and do not discard.)

For those new to the field, it is encouraging to know that it is not too difficult to organize support groups. Normally, people will come to you with their suggestions. Local hospitals or health agencies can be a great help in providing facilitators and referrals. It's mostly a matter of you providing the space and helping to get the word out about your support group. If there is a need for it, clients will come.

OTHER PROGRAMS TO CONSIDER

Adult Day Care

Senior day care programs are proliferating rapidly in communities all over the country, and some of them are being located within a senior center or residential facility. As the name implies, these programs provide day care for older people unable to make it to your center on their own. Typically, these programs include door-to-door transportation, a meal, a modified exercise program, arts and crafts, and most importantly, an opportunity to socialize with other seniors.

There are two types of adult day care programs. The first, usually referred to as a day health care center (or a "medical model" day care program), is intended to serve the more severely disabled type of client (for instance, one with Alzheimer's or some other serious form of brain impairment or someone confined to a wheelchair). To serve these very dependent clients, the day health care center must have on staff an R. N. and other medically oriented professionals, such as an occupational therapist and a physical therapist. Normally, a day health care center requires a state license to operate and is eligible for Medicaid reimbursement. For elders not eligible for Medicaid, the private care fee can go as high as $50 per day at such facilities. Most centers offer a sliding fee.

The other type of day care facility, referred to as a "social model" day care center, is intended for the less severely disabled older person. Typically, the clients are capable of getting around by themselves, even if they have to use a walker or cane. They are continent and not afflicted with latter-stage Alzheimer's or some equally disabling physical or mental handicap. However, they are unable to drive or even board public transit unassisted. Clients of social day care programs generally do not need the level of care offered by a day health facility, but they cannot, on their own, take advantage of the services offered at a senior center. Fees at a social day care center are lower than those set for day health programs because medical staff is not required. On the other hand, normally the services offered at a social day care program are not reimbursable by Medicaid. Licensing requirements vary from state to state.

The vast majority of both medical and social model day care programs are located outside of, rather than within, senior center facilities. The rationale for this separation is the special attention and care that must be given to disabled older people. The argument goes that very frail older people will feel more comfortable with others in the same boat and can more easily be given the personal care they require. Also relevant, though sometimes unspoken, is the conventional wisdom that the healthy, younger seniors will not feel comfortable sharing space with the very frail.

A number of aging professionals favor a more integrated approach, locating their adult day care program within an existing senior center or residence. This approach, they point out, has the advantage of encouraging healthy seniors to volunteer to assist their more frail peers. When seniors help seniors in this manner, a wholesome atmosphere is created at the center. People feel useful and good about themselves when they are able to contribute their time to such a program. An additional advantage of locating the day care component within an existing senior facility is the availability of so many other services. Day care participants have access to various special events at the senior center, arts and crafts activities, classes, and health-related services already provided to the general senior population.

Respite Programs

As the number of at risk seniors increases, family members taking care of a dependent elder at home are asking senior facilities to provide "granny or grandpa sitting" services. Their request for respite programs is not surprising, given the burden of 24-hour care. Even the most compassionate caregivers need some time to themselves, for their own sakes as well as for their charges. It is a godsend to have a place away from home where both the cared for and the caregiver can have some space and time away from one another.

Respite programs are often similar to social day care programs in terms of what is offered, e.g., a meal, recreational activities, arts and crafts, etc. But the focus of respite care is on the caregiver. The name says it all. Furthermore, respite services differ widely in scope from community to community. A respite program can be offered for as little as one evening or afternoon a month and staffed entirely by volunteers. No fees are involved. Transportation and a bag lunch are provided by the caregivers. Even this minimum service is greatly appreciated by caregivers who are stressed to their limits by the demands of full-time patient care. Some senior centers offer more formal programs of respite three or four times a week and charge a sliding fee for the service.

In starting a respite service at your center, we recommend that you begin modestly with a once or twice monthly program. Once you get a better feel for the need and for your requirements, you can expand it. The local Area Agency on Aging may be able to advise you and possibly offer start-up funds, if necessary. In some communities, local service clubs take on the responsibility of "granny and grandpa sitting" as a volunteer project. You will need to set your own guidelines as to the level of care you can offer. For example, you probably won't be in a position to accept incontinent clients or those with more severe brain impairment. You will also need to check with your insurance carrier to make sure you have liability coverage. But, all things considered, respite care is one of the easiest and most needed services you can offer. The payoff in community goodwill is incalculable.

7 *Programming for the 50-60 Generation*

A WISE MAN ONCE IMPLIED THAT BY evaluating the significant historical events of the world during the decade in which you were ten to twenty years of age, you may discover what it is that excites you, frightens you, and the events that have shaped the values by which you live. As the Baby Boomers come of age to become senior center participants, you will discover rock-'n'-roll, tightly scheduled lives, and sandwich generation children. The 50-year-old individual experienced Viet Nam, "sex, drugs, and rock-'n'-roll," single parent families, and cross-country separation of extended family life. By evaluating the components of the fifty-something person's life, you may just discover the direction your senior center program should take to meet the needs of this group and to greet them with programs that will entice them into your facility.

One of the first challenges you will discover in developing programs for this age group is an attitude. All during the life of this "new senior," he/she has been bombarded with messages of the importance of youth—and senior centers are for "old" people. If your center and its programs have that "granny smell," you may just have to get creative. Who says you are trapped within the four walls of your center? Who says you can only be open 8 a.m. - 5 p.m.? Who says bingo, crafts, and pool have to be the only type of recreation programs you offer? This new generation of seniors is more sophisticated, more challenging, and more open (than that)!

THE SANDWICH GENERATION

Perhaps your first interaction with the young senior will be for help with an "aging" parent. When clearly evaluated this situation often reveals two sets of dilemmas: (1) getting help for the older parent and (2) meeting the needs of the child— the new senior. Obviously, having on hand a good information and referral program and knowing how to access information in other parts of the country will go a long way in helping both parties in this instance. Yet what about the ongoing stress felt by the child as he/she deals with a failing parent? They, too, are seniors and should receive assistance from you as an aging services professional. One program which is working well in many locales is to hold "Sandwich Generation Seminars," workshops designed to equip family members with information on how to access resources, to take care of legal concerns, to encourage sharing, and to provide support for those trying to cope with the difficult decisions caused by caring for an aging and/or ailing parent. Thought must be put into the time and place you hold this program, as many of the senior children needing assistance are still working. Try offering a one day intensive on a Saturday or holding a series of brown-bag lunches at the site of a large local employer.

Evening sessions over a period of several weeks have also worked well.

Make sure, too, that your presenters are knowledgeable in the field. Poor information or lack of information will come back to haunt you. The new senior, especially with an ailing parent, has no time to waste.

PRERETIREMENT PLANNING

Another component of the fifty-something person's life is his/her work-life and the knowledge that it will come to an end. As an aging services professional, you are an avenue for making the transition smoother. You can facilitate the preretirement process by creating an understanding (through services you offer) of where the preretiree stands financially, socially, physically, and mentally.

Many (hopefully most) senior centers have a network of both public and private service providers who are willing to donate their time to speak, do one-on-one consultations, etc. Why not put together a preretirement package?

Package A:

Develop a regularly scheduled time (quarterly) during which the preretiree can come to your facility and receive a broad overview of the services available in your community that can be tapped when they are needed. The format can be any you choose, but once again be conscious that you are marketing to the working folk. In-depth information, given professionally and in a short amount of time, will sell and be remembered. A round robin workshop has done wonders for some communities. Also, don't forget to include the senior center itself when you are considering resources to participate in this program. You can tailor volunteer opportunities, offer hobby and interest programs that cross the work/retirement barrier, fill in any empty hours with interesting new learning concepts, offer a place to relax and make new friends, and/or you can whisk the new retiree away to new places and new adventures.

Package B:

Work with large local employers or merchant associations to develop their own in-house assessments for those nearing retirement. You are probably the key they have been looking for to access local resources. Be careful—this is not the place to compete with retired employee expertise. If, for example, the company offers insurance counseling, don't bring in your HICAP (Health Insurance Counseling & Advocacy Program) worker.

The retired company official who volunteers his time is much more familiar with that company's insurance plans. Your job is to look wider still and find the loopholes with which even great employers can't help.

Package C:

Put all the knowledge you have together in a handbook or folder that can be presented to those who are entering the second half of life. You will be surprised at the amount of knowledge you and your staff have to offer. These information packets can be distributed at your center, by business personnel departments, at the Chamber of Commerce, at doctor's offices, etc. Get local merchants and service providers to buy into the printing cost and use a format that is readily changed as your community evolves. These packets will become an invaluable tool for you as well as for those in your neighborhood that are retiring.

I'M YOUNG, HEALTHY, AND READY TO WORK

A most familiar and often frustrating scene has just occurred at your reception desk. A fifty-something generation individual has discovered that the lawn can only be mowed twice per week, that the holes on the golf course are looking too familiar, and his/her spouse is getting on his/her nerves. This individual wants and needs something constructive to do. He/she wants to volunteer! How do you react? Do you think to yourself, and subconsciously transmit the message of, "Oh no, not another one. We don't have any more good or ongoing volunteer jobs!"? Do you say to yourself, "This person will never last. They will fly to Hawaii next week and want to come in at 8 a.m. one day and 3 p.m. the next"? Do you unleash your creativity and truly welcome them with open arms because you have a list of program goals you and your advisory group want achieved by energetic, willing-to-learn, creative, and skilled talent?

Good volunteer jobs are jobs. They require descriptions, project goals, and management. You will do yourself, your agency, and your volunteer pool (both potential and actual) a big favor by taking time to put on paper the general action plan to achieve the "impossible dreams." "I don't have time" you say—so make it a priority to take advantage of situations handed to you. Take ten minutes to fill that young senior in on your dreams and to ask him/her what he/she really would like to do. If there is even a hint of a match, make an appointment to cultivate an action plan. You can create meaningful and challenging volunteer opportunities and meet your goals, too. Note: if you truly cannot find a match of talents and needs, have a list of other agencies the individual might contact or refer them to your regional RSVP (Retired Senior Volunteer Program).

LOOKING FOR FRIENDS

Another phenomena, which often happens during mid-life and as one leaves the work world to enter the retirement years is the decline of social contacts. This potential isolation can be deterred during the fifty-something years by establishing a different, nonwork-related social circle. As a senior center director, you can facilitate new relationships by offering contact generating social functions. You can create a good mix of participants by hosting cheese and wine socials, dinner clubs, and/or weekend brunch gatherings. These events can simply be a social gathering or can feature light entertainment. Be creative with your locale—the senior center may not be the best place to host such a group. Advertising the activity itself (not promoting the senior center) may also serve to generate more attendance for you.

TAKE ME AWAY

How many times have you heard someone say, "When I was in college (younger), I liked to climb mountains, ride a bike, raft rivers, jump a train, but I haven't done it in years" or "I always wanted to try that, but the kids were too young or I couldn't get away or I didn't have the money," etc? There is no (good) reason why the healthy fifty-something senior cannot take part in these activities. You can be the driving force to "get back to the basics of fun."

After checking with your insurance carrier and risk management, get out of those four walls you work within or at least send those young seniors outdoors. Facilitate adventure type activities by hooking up interested folks to biking, hiking, skiing, or flying enthusiast groups in your area. Organize a small group to visit the chapter meeting or to have a club representative come to you.

Another option to get people moving is to contact a travel agency that specializes in group "adventure touring"—trips that add an active ingredient such as marlin fishing, spelunking, or flightseeing to the itinerary upon arrival at the destination. If you can't find a company to plan the adventure part of the tour, contact the concierge at the hotel at which you are staying. They will know the local hot air balloon operator, rafting company, knowledgeable wilderness guide, or city tour leader *extraordinaire.*

If staying closer to home is more realistic, taking a nature walk through (and really seeing) the local cow pasture, junk hunting along the railroad tracks, or experiencing the sensation of skyscrapers all around you can provide for a sense of risk-taking and escape.

A PASSION FOR SPORTS

Swimming, golf, tennis, aerobics, volleyball, softball—the sports activities we have grown up with and love should remain a valued part of active retirement especially for the 50 - 60-year-old in good health. Even though those who are active in these physical fitness realms are most likely connected to facilities which can provide the services they need, it behooves the senior center professional to actively provide for or join forces with others to provide for the continuation of these activities. By working with the staff of other city facilities or by "working deals" with the YMCA or local fitness center, you can facilitate lower cost sessions, spice up the competition by sponsoring a tournament, and, at the same time, get your foot into the door of the 50 - 60 age market. Your name will quickly be recognized not just as a caretaker of the more frail, but as a promoter of healthy active senior years.

The truly devoted, competition-minded, older athlete can also be served by you. This person is probably looking for fair and challenging competition. Getting that individual involved with, or to help in the organization of, a local-level "Senior Olympics" may be the tool to reach this special segment of the population. Your event, planned properly, may even draw out the former Olympic athlete or world champion or those who almost made the team. Information on how to organize this type of event is available through the National Senior Sports Foundation. In becoming involved, you will have shaped a few muscles, sharpened the mental game, and provided an opportunity for the active older adult to share the dreams of glory in athletic competition. The ongoing challenge to be the best, despite the odds, is strong within us all.

A TIME TO LEARN

Not only does the body need exercise, but so does the mind if it is to remain clear. The 50 - 60-year-old may want to stretch in new directions after years of work or homemaking. Perhaps they have put off exploring a new philosophy, researching a hobby, examining social issues, or sharpening an academic skill because "there was never enough time."

The options for senior center managers to facilitate learning opportunities are as broad as the profession. You may simply refer someone to the local college or adult school, contract someone to teach at your site, or with significant interest you may wish to take on the challenge of offering a workshop or ongoing class yourself. You may even challenge a volunteer to strengthen his or her abilities by teaching.

Don't rule out any subject. You will be surprised at what captures people's interests. If you "don't have a clue" as to where to begin, conduct a survey or take a ride on the shirt-tails of a local event. In one community alone, an international volleyball tournament featuring teams from South America spawned an interest in basic Spanish, an annual antique sale invited a course in collecting and appraising "old junk," and rapid growth sparked a series of pre-election lectures on environmental impact reports, city planning methods, endangered species laws, and more.

By offering education opportunities to the 50 - 60-year-old and better, you instill a sense of the future and the joy of accomplishing that which was long put off. You will challenge the mind to keep growing and stretching.

In acknowledgement of the facts and in conclusion, it is important to take note that most likely the fifty-something generation programs you create are not going to be (at least at first) your most well-attended functions. This is a tough group to market. Your newsletter isn't going to do it, the newspaper game is questionable, and employers aren't always real cooperative. However, in many instances, you are mandated to, and we should all be compelled to, reach the new young senior population. They are the key to our ongoing success, our task force for future programming, and the fastest-growing segment of the population. The fifty-something crowd is not going to go away—they are going to multiply. So put on those cross-trainers and "play hard" as you "just do it."

We've come to the end of a beginning. In *Beyond Bingo,* we hope we have stirred up your creative juices and made you think of that whole world of new programs waiting to be initiated by senior recreation pros like yourselves.

Now, it's up to you to both try some of the ideas we've shared with you and to come up with new programs, alternative services that all of us can implement in the months and years ahead.

Many of you, by your comments and suggestions, have helped us write this book. We invite you to continue to share with us any ideas you tried (or dreamed of trying) at your senior center or residence. We are planning a follow-up to *Beyond Bingo* and would enjoy incorporating program suggestions from throughout the country.

Send your ideas to the co-author listed below. We'll give you credit and you'll have the satisfaction of sharing your brainstorm with thousands of your fellow professionals in aging.

We hope you enjoyed reading *Beyond Bingo* as much as we enjoyed writing it.

Send your idea(s) to the address below. We will be happy to hear from you, and your contribution(s) will be greatly appreciated.

Sal Arrigo, Jr.
Senior Center Director
Cordova Senior Center
Cordova Recreation and Park District
3480 Routier Road
Sacramento, CA 95827

Related Books from Venture Publishing

The Activity Gourmet
  by Peggy Powers

The Game Finder: A Leader's Guide to Great Activities
  by Annette C. Moore

Great Special Events and Activities
  by Annie Morton, Angie Prosser and Sue Spangler

Leisure Education: A Manual of Activities and Resources
  by Norma J. Stumbo and Steven R. Thompson

Leisure Education II: More Activities and Resources
  by Norma J. Stumbo

Recreation Programming And Activities For Older Adults
  by Jerold E. Elliott and Judith A. Sorg-Elliott